Sarita Khullar

Scattered Blooms

ROOM9 PUBLICATIONS
www.artoonsinn.com

Copyright Details

First Edition 2026
ISBN: 9788198431271

Cover Design by Mithru Rachamalla
Illustrations by Srivalli Rekha
Interior Design by Srivalli Rekha

Published by ArtoonsInn Room9 Publications
Printed in India by ArtoonsInn

ArtoonsInn Room9 Publications
www.room9publications.com

Dedication

To my mother, Mrs. Sudesh Khurana, whose mellifluous singing wafted through the house while she did her chores and still has a calming effect.

My father, Prof. D. R. Khurana, who believed that every kind of creative art was merely a wastage of time, yet quoted Rumi and Ghalib, listened to Farida Khanum, and read me the stories of Tolstoy and Maupassant.

My siblings, who made my childhood wonderful and continue to add cheer. To my uncle, Sh. S. K. Malik, for inspiring me with his superb writing, and who called me a "late bloomer."

My husband, Dr. Ashok Khullar, for tolerating my drawbacks and supporting me in every way. To my friends and family, who keep me afloat during stressful times.

My friend and publisher, Mithru Rachamalla, for his amazing patience with my lack of technical skill and my procrastination.

Srivalli Rekha, my friend and an eminent poet herself, for helping to illustrate and edit the anthology.

Dr. Pamela Bedi, for reading and reviewing all my poems.

Ranjit Narayanan, for his reviews, help, and honest criticism.

Husna Thaslim, Pallavi Suri, Mallika Verma, Natasha Sequeira, Mumtaz Khorakiwala, Debashree Basak and Moonmoon Chaudhury for their love and support.

To all the poets and readers of ArtoonsInn Poetry Parlour, for their encouragement and love. And to all the readers who may find an echo of their own passions in the lyrics that I have woven.

To my children and grandchildren who constantly remained a source of inspiration.

I shall be eternally thankful.

-Sarita Khullar

Blooms in order

History and Poetry

History, the prerogative of the winners,
Written mostly by flatterers and sycophants,
Is half-truth, distorted largely to please;
While real heroes are forgotten with ease,
Poetry, the language of hearts and humanity,
Since eternity sings of subtle human reality,
Songs of joy, loneliness, adulation or prayers,
Each nuance of love, each sting of betrayal,
Shades of morning sky, hues of setting sun,
In poesy true reflections of our mind we discern,
Making us wonder how could the poets know,
What sensitive hearts feel even now yet cannot show.

□□□□

Songsters of Spring

Eerie silence of the winter fades by and by,
Now these dulcet melodies of springtime spy,
A lone robin on a budding bough twitters,
Lovely red cardinal and blue jay add to lyrics,
Listen to mellifluous orchestra of flinches, warbles,
It is Lark's secret symphony that fills the air.
While the Nightingale's sweet note sound shrill and fair,
Honey bees hum to nascent ecstatic blooms,
While the grasshopper sings in a piercing tone,
Sparrows chirp and cheep announcing the advent of dawn,
Sweet music flows uninterrupted in the Nature's Lawn.

□□□□

Life

A panorama of images that quickly pass,
Through the casement of a slow moving train,
Life goes on in a dream like trance,
Blurred at times, sometimes manifest.
All that we see is a dream within a dream,
Vast sea of serenity or deep waters of pain,
Lovely flowers of spring or winter's harsh rain,
Colours of twilight that ever changing remain,
Innocent giggles of carefree childhood,
Like patchwork by friends on the bridal quilt,
Mystic nature at every step changing her stance,
A passionate romance or happy dance.

□□□□

Motherhood

I remember your very first cry, my child,
A relief that you have finally arrived,
Touched the hands so soft and tiny,
You were taking in your first breaths still;
Just a flash of sudden thrill filled my heart,
We talked of joy you brought in our lives,
Like the moon you brightened our nights,
Forgetting the clock or time's restraint,
You became your father's and my only plan,
Our lives revolved round you, simple and plain,
Everything else didn't matter again,
The morning lighted up with your smiles,
And as night fell in you we took delight,
I will and can never think of another,
No treasure could have made us happier.
Who can make us rejoice and keep our lives so full and well!

□□□□

Lost Prayers

Where do all the prayers go,
Coming out of wounded souls,
Of helpless and innocent people,
Standing at Devil's threshold?
Devastated cities and homes,
Scattered limbs of the dead,
Excruciating cries of the wounded,
Why fall on ears callous and deaf?
Birds and beasts lying at the altar,
Of human cruelty, lust and greed,
They too pray to the unheeding sky,
To save them from devilish mob,
Pray we all and pray we must,
When fate and fortunes deceive,
Karma says you get what you deserve,
But isn't it a thing hard to believe?
Let our sincere prayers waft high,
For a world undivided, without pain,
Where evil thoughts don't come nigh,
Let compassion and love remain.

□□□□

Farewell Hope

For days together I can smile on,
Lingering onto the last thread of hope,
Tolerating pain, yet thinking it will go,
Waiting at the edge for miracles to happen,
Now when life is slipping by,
Like sand from my cupped hands,
No more my eyes can hold the tears,
I give out a desperate cry,
Helpless, weak and hopeless,
Perhaps there is no one to listen,
Perhaps I will die a thousand deaths,
Before reaching your threshold,
Where in my imagination.
You are waiting to greet me,
Away from the pain and sufferings,
Amongst the haze of my tears,
Undulating like ocean waves,
Hope is dying down,
Like the rays of setting sun,
Waving goodbye through my balcony.

□□□□

Vibrant Spring...

Cold cruel winter covered in white shroud,
Benumbed senses and troubled breath loud,
Making the swans leave from the hedge.
Flying up to earth's remotest edge,
Sorrows of life are depicted in winter,
Glorious year in a painful whimper.
Suddenly a new garb dons the earth,
A new hope sprouts amidst glee and mirth,
From the chilly winter, sprightly spring takes birth,
With the earth painted with greenest hue,
Adorned with beauty is every view.
Life moves on at its sweetest pace,
Neither pain nor joy remains long in the race.

□□□□

LOVE: A Sly Hunter

Imperceptibly I moved towards the lifeless wall,
You tried to hear my footsteps like an experienced sniper,
Filling my innocent mind with fear,
For I know who are shot with darts of Cupid,
Can't call themselves either live or dead,
I remember your sweet nothings have semblance of truth,
Your promises are like mad temptations.
You will let me live in fractions only,
My youth will be spent in believing your lies,
You remain dominant and I blindly walk behind.
Nobody does trust your love,
But bravely I bear others' jeers and taunts,
I am a mesmerised fool I wish to be yours,
Delicately I love you with my mind and soul,
I became a part of your mesmerising aura,
I glorify now in the glory of your light!

□□□□

Swan Song

Silence all melodies of nature,
Mellifluous birds or trickle of drops,
For my love has gone to distant land,
You too leave me alone and bother me not,
Let life slog on its monotonous path,
Shut all cheerful musical tones,
I don't want to live on any more,
For, without you, mine is an empty existence
Now that love is gone nothing gives me consolation.
Lock all the windows and doors.
Let me make it as gloomy as my heart,
Darkness inside is like a solitary confinement,
Utter darkness outside will make no difference.
You can lock out all beauty, love and cheer,
Let life take a flight to the path unclear,
I can still feel the ecstasy of your love,
But it's the last lament of my agonised soul,
Now it's time to sing my swan song!!

□□□□

Magic

Roses bloomed into faded cheeks,
Increasing the palpitation of an indifferent heart,
Colouring heart's landscape in a thousand hues,
Love, you are a miracle imperceptibly coming to view,

Breathing life into a sepulchral stone,
A strange happiness that all sorrows atone,
Arousing all passions of the heart,
Where did thou learn this magical art?

□□□□

Delicate Twigs of Hope

Dark ominous clouds camouflage the golden sun,
Pouring rain has drenched my dreams to pulp,
Cruel winds lash fiercely against my casement,
Torrential beat of waves is heard from the gulf,
Striving to intrude my cosy castle of dreams,
With trembling lips I pray for your well-being,
My palpitating heart stumbles many a times,
Twigs of hope I collect to kindle my tender evening.
Expecting my moon to grace my heart's horizon,
At every sound I run to peer through the glass of life,
Wiping mist of doubt with the warmth of my love,
The mist that lingers gloomily on my very being,
When no firefly glows in the moonless night,
Not even a single star glows to brighten my path,
These twigs of hope will light the bonfire of bliss,
Sanguine fire will thaw passions dormant and chill!

□□□□

Birds in the Backyard

As soon as I fill the bird feeder,
They arrive fluttering their colourful wings,
Coming from nowhere these invisible fairies,
Transform and change into lively birds.
Who colours them with the brightest hues?
Red cardinals, black birds and jays blue,
Wood peckers with different colours,
Goldfinches with shades of yellow,
Colour my mind with such wondrous glow.
Look, naughty agile squirrel.
Becomes a spoil sport, when it jumps,
Directly on bird's feeder and scares,
Little winged angels quickly hide,
In tall pines, magnolias and oaks,
All the grain spilled down by the squirrel,
Is picked up by the scurrying chipmunks,
Since the birds are hidden in thick trees,
Scared of eagles, soaring overhead,
But slowly they come again,
To enliven my backyard.

□□□□

Verses

Fragrant blooms of human garth of emotions,
Little strings of beauty, from Chaucer to moderns,
With flowering rhythm, set in rhyme or free,
A sparkling diamond to the bejewelled literature tree.
Humbly expressing thoughts of a powerful preacher.
Or call it the babbling of a lunatic mind,
Or a genius brain's powerful insight,
Crying in desperation over loss of love or life,
A glimpse captured of the fleeting beauty,
As if from an expert photographer's lens,
Surviving in the words for the ages to come.
A firefly held loosely in the fist, illuminating,
A charismatic rainbow as the downpour ends,
All the love and all the pain,
All the losses all the gain,
All weird and wonderful moments of life,
Captured beautifully in rhythm and rhyme,
A fresh cool breeze for the burning heart,
A solace when life turns sour and tart,
Generations of wisdom, seeds of revolution,
Inspiration to live, daring to seek adventure
Delicate feelings expressing our joys and care.

□□□□

Undelivered Letters

Treasure lies in the silken box of heart,
Filled to seams, of gems and jewels,
Of my unuttered words and unsung songs,
Each precious tear I shed for you,
Is etched in these undelivered letters,
It will open like Pandora's Box,
The world will be strewn with petals soft,
Of colours mesmerising, hues of love,
Enchanting fragrance wafting like turtle dove,
Celebrating celestial passions supreme,
Stricken heart pens a letter every time,
Waits for an answer in nightly dreams,
Alas! My dream turns to savage nightmare,
Lonely it waits, noiselessly it screams?
For the balmy touch of unseen gleam.
I wait at the casement of dying day,
A sepulchral figure silhouetted in spray,
With some faith and flicker of hope,
If not in this birth, in the next or next,
Letters will reach you in floral envelope.

□□□□

Sparrows

Throwing back puffed rice, while leaving her *mayka*,
Wrapped in red attire, hands decorated in henna,
Wistfully looking back at her childhood home,
Every Punjabi bride sang the song of sparrows,
Teary eyed telling the parents of their long flight,
Their tiny wings taking them to unknown destinations.
The song lingers but the sparrows are gone,
Leaving our courtyards and souls forlorn.
Would sit in dozens in our veranda swings,
Some drenched and fluffy drying out their wings,
Sprinkling drops of water around, stuttering like kings.
Talking in chirps, pecking at the grain we spread,
"Shhhh," just sit quiet or they will fly away in rain,
Mother will warn us about this time and again.
"Don't eat like a sparrow, was the advice we got,
"Naughty like sparrows," when we jumped a lot,
"Don't switch on the fan," was a forceful cry,
For the little chicks have just learnt to fly.
Invaded every room and roosted there at night,
Waking up everyone before taking day's flight,
Murmuration they started like honey bees from the hives,
Tiny gray/ brown birds ruled our homes and lives,
Loved and treated like little girls sweet and sophisticated,
With their sweet chirps our hearts they dominated.
Then one day I found one dead in a flower vase,

Then another, yet another, there was no pause,
Things were just the same, no dearth of food or water,
What caused them to die still was a matter of wonder.
Two mobile towers had come up near our place,
To these the mystery of disaster we could trace,
Years have gone by; I rarely see these birds of delight,
One day we will regret to think, we caused such a plight.

□□□□

*Mayka: Parents' home

Just Woman

A Super Woman? Nay!
I am just woman!
I am fractured and flawed,
Still I am fantastic,
I fumble and tumble,
Yet I am fabulous!
Man!
Can you resist my smile?
Can you tolerate my tears?
I am a promise of love,
Forever and ever.
A darling daughter, an adorable sister,
Mother divine or a sweetheart!
Defying norms,
I rise from the dust,
Where you throw me and forget,
For I am the seed,
Nurtured by vehement struggles,
Breaking out of torturous ground,
A Laxmi Bai or Hazrat Begum
A tiny voice of rebellion,
A timid Rosa refusing the seat,
A Mother Lu fighting Han Dynasty,
Sugula, the rebel Queen fearless,
Maybe I am a girl next door,

Resisting lecherous gaze of lust,
A bride refusing demands unjust,
Marie Curie fighting all odds,
Working for greater human cause,
Not all could make it,
To see the light of the day,
Many did struggle,
And were lost in the way,
Why don't you consider common woman,
Someone asked Cartoonist Laxman!
"I had so far never seen such woman,
Each woman I saw is a special one."

□□□□

A Child's Pain

They dragged me out of the rubble,
Of what once was our home,
We all ran I don't know where,
But why was the little one left there?
Mother cried, "*Let me put a handful of dust over him.*"
No time, run, run!
We were cramped in a truck
That sped to nowhere,
Hungry and exhausted, bewildered,
With parched throats and glazed eyes we moved,
Yet, no one dared to utter a moan.
A river to cross and another was lost,
Quietly we watched him drown from the cliff.
Our sister was dragged and left for dead,
A living corpse she remained since then.
Mother shed silent tears this time, and moved with human river,
Casting a quick glance behind,
Pitched tents were our home now,
Stood in the queue for food and water
Laughed at by the people there,
For, our funny ways and funny language
Lecherous glances and lewd remarks
Mother ignored for our sake,
She doesn't cry anymore,
Never again I heard her laugh,
Patiently we are bearing the brunt of,
Ambitions of politicians and so called lords.

Ocean Waves

Soft it is like the morning dew,
Yet my love is intense,
Like that of the ocean waves
Calm, serene,
Imperceptibly advancing,
Making, breaking,
Rejected it returns,
Strives again,
Sometimes smoothly, calmly,
Like a patient lover,
Sometimes agitated,
Mad in the love of an indifferent shore,
Agitated like strong bellows it strikes,
To gain an iota of love,
At times mad crazy like Tsunami,
Destroying everything that comes its way,
For love is madness,
That knows no reason.
And the shore!
Indifferent, calm,
Doesn't even know that,
Still steadily it is succumbing to
My crazy love,
And becoming a part of me.

□□□□

An Abandoned Abode

An abandoned house on my way to work,
Every day I spy its magnificent architecture.
With boundary walls blackened by algae,
Ravaged by the vagaries of sun and rain,
Though still magnificent in every aspect.
I think of the people, who lived here,
Children playing in the arched veranda,
This lawn with old mango trees must have,
Reverberated with their innocent laughter,
Now strewn with weeds and vines spatter.
Sun rays through the coloured glass panes,
A row of faded red pillars in the veranda,
Bring alive in my mind those lively people,
Sitting on a swing or a woven *charpai*,
Chopping vegetables for lunch or dinner,
Playing *antakshari* in melodious sing song.
Or might be playing a game of carrom or ludo,
A lively game of cards amidst accusations,
And cards being thrown by the one who lost,
Followed by loud laughter from the winners.
I haven't peeped inside but I can think of.
Old mahogany dining table with finest china,
A delicate plate, cup still lying inside cupboard,
All protected securely by spiders' gossamer web,
And dusted with nature's free flowing dust.
I imagine alcoves to keep old statues and,
Nooks for candles, tiny vases and ornaments.

A wooden horse still rocking to and fro,
As though a child has just come down,
Kept in a corner while the children grew.
I have been watching it for years now,
A strong urge to get down the rickshaw,
And explore that mystic house comes & goes,
I am always in a hurry to reach the college
I am always in a hurry to go back home,
This abandoned house haunts my soul,
And lonely parents when children were gone.

□□□□

Charpai: A traditional woven bed used in South Asian countries.

Antakshari: A musical parlour game where the participants sing a song starting with the last word/ letter of the previous song.

Dying Hope

Eastern sky is painted with alpenglow,
New dawn brings fresh hues of hope,
Silly heart peeping through the glass
Waits eagerly for the love it lost.
Memories haunt throughout the day,
Like sepia prints of old photographs,
Perchance seen in an old album,
Making one laugh and cry at once.
Life is going on amidst pain and loss,
A deep vacuum your absence has caused,
Hope diminishing as each day wears off,
Still like a sharp thorn in my soul it has paused.
The Orange orb now dips in the ocean,
Sad elongated silhouettes dot the glade,
My hope dies slowly with the dying day,
Teary eyed, I watch even my shadows fade

□□□□

Facade

My silent face no expression shows,
Of smouldering fire that inside glows,
That scalds me and doesn't let me live,
In thousand pieces it's ready to rive,
An innocent heart that loved so pure.
Don't go by my ever smiling eyes,
They have learnt to tell many a lies,
An ocean of bitter tears they hold,
Showing on the outside appearance bold,
Lips don't part to talk of days bygone,
Of a soul now dreary and all alone,
I know well that no one hears,
The tale of love, pain and tears.

□□□□

The Peacock at the Zoo

This rain so vibrant, so lively.
Reminds me of the peacock;
Lonely and bound in a small enclosure,
In the world class Hyderabad zoo,
Boasting of humane treatment to animal kind.
No love for that lonely bird did it find.
At the first shower of the summer rain,
Delighted with lovely cool breeze,
He opened his wings to charm a hen,
Enthralled visitors on the track did freeze.
His thrilled spirit for a moment forgot,
He was bound in a cramped pen/ space,
I could imagine him thinking of the forest,
Where he had spent time with his brood,
Those pleasant days, those magical nights,
When he lived away from man's fright.

□□□□

Parting

Let me linger on,
For a few more seconds,
In my old house, nay home,
Let me peep out of the windows,
And see where bulbuls made their nests,
Watch the downpour that washes verdant lawns,
Allow me to move from room to room humming,
A happy tune that comes naturally from a heart,
That has known love and given it back in abundance,
Before I go far away to a place where strangers live,
Where the mind will be dull and foggy,
In the absence of loved ones turned strangers,
Don't push me away with your loveless glances,
Let me smell the dusty curtains and sit for a moment,
On the rocking chair where I had spent many evenings,
Watching my little dog frolicking and chasing tiny birds,
Go I will…

But let me shed a few tears at the familiar threshold.

Mother

Mother! How I loved you.
For standing for me,
For wiping my tears,
For saving me from scolding,
Of grandma and papa.

How I loved you for doing my work,
Getting me ready for the school,
For healing my bruises,
With a gentle pat and kiss,
Telling me stories that I still miss.

How I hated you for searching my almirah,
For capturing my lies before I uttered,
For picking and choosing my friends,
For stopping me to attend parties,
With friends you didn't like.

How I hated you to read my face.
And confront me for sins I wished to hide
For making me blurt out the truth.
Howsoever hard I tried to hide it.
With penetrating eyes you bared me all

How I missed you after my marriage,
With aliens all around the place,
For whom I was a slave they bought.

With no feelings or a single thought,
A part of my being there I lost.

How I missed your fun and wit,
With sorrow, grief openly writ,
On my whole being,
I dragged on, could not complain,
Didn't want to hurt or give you pain.

Life passed thus and you were gone.
Silently I shed tears silently I moan,
Still hear your songs sweetly sung,
That waft around me like fragrance,
And brighten my moments dark and grim!

□□□□

Childhood Secrets

Long hot summer vacations, never ending noon,
A bane for harassed mother, for us a boon,
Forced were we to stay at home,
Keep ourselves safe from the angry yellow sun,
Who in a jiffy could our lovely soft skin burn,
But little rascals as we were, will some prank devise,
Pampering the maid and scaling the wall,
Would reach neighbouring mango trees tall,
Then coming back with our pile of fruit,
With palpitating hearts hiding the loot,
Excitedly chattered my sister and me,
With movements soft and inaudible speed,
Of joys and fears of afternoon mischief?
And a sound less loud than our heartbeat,
When caught red handed, would shed silent tears,
A little bit of scolding would never a lesson teach!

□□□□

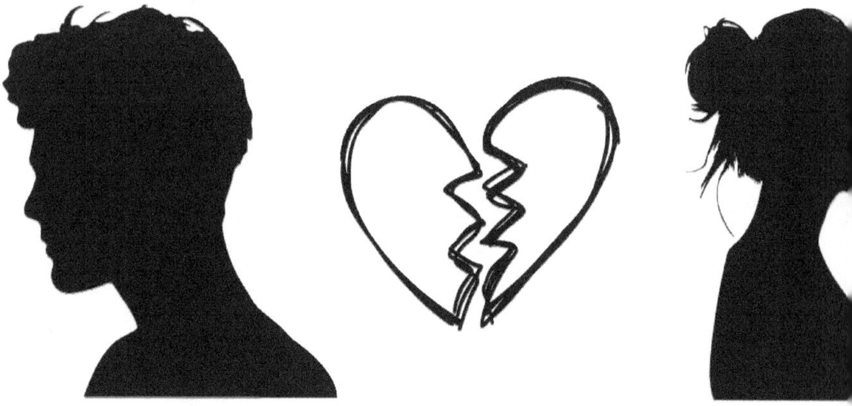

Sacred Passion

I don't blame you,
You never made any promise,
Just entered my life unnoticed,
Walked beside me without a word,
When I met you, no memory I have,
Imprisoned for life, found no escape.
Your music vibrates in my heart now,
Your fragrance intoxicates my being.
No more I am able to alienate myself,
From the magic you weaved,
Benumbed my senses, had my logic shorn,
Oblivious, unconscious, madly I roam.
Sacred and pious as the thought divine
My heart will hold this passion sublime.

□□□□

Days Bygone

When I am unable to sleep at night,
And the day takes ages to dawn,
My heart takes me to the lanes,
Where I spent my days bygone
Long unkempt hair or a ponytail,
A lovely frock getting small and small,
Hopping or jumping or playing ball,
Running around till about to fall.
Arguing over trifles and forgetting soon,
Slipping out slyly in the hot afternoon,
Ravaging every fruit tree all around,
Will not stop till scolded sound.
Pretending to study in a silent space,
Sharing stories of the school that slowly fade,
Laughing at teachers, mocking class mates,
Falling silent again at father's voice enraged.
Giggling softly, talking ever so slow,
Our faces had the loveliest glow.
Long lost is the togetherness and love,
That we shared in our childhood home,
Those lovely days and blessed nights,
Sleeping soundly after play or fights,
Wish those carefree days are back,
To compensate for love and sleep I lack.

□□□□

Love Hurts

I lie here choking,
From the barbs of destiny
Where the love turns sour,
And life hurts more than blisters,
Or by a thousand prickly thorns

□□□□

#Tanka

Beware!

Waiting at night, near a lonely casement,
Overlooking a path where no travellers pass by,
A lone shepherd is sometimes seen searching,
A wayward sheep that wandered too far away,
And lost its way in deepest recesses of this woodland,
The grove that all the mystic forces hold, living or dead,
Benevolent or evil, secret, unrevealed, unknown.
That is the forest of my lonely heart,
Inhabited by dreadful beasts of hatred,
Fear, envy, anger, gnawing at it night and day
Making it hurt and bleed at its misfortunes.
Awaiting its lonely shepherd, the love!
An unknown voice echoes in my mind,
Ringing warning bells of impending danger,
Beware! Beware! O heart of alluring love,
It will kill not, but won't let you live.

□□□□

Distant Dream

You are not mine,
But you are a part of my dream world,
A spec of stardust,
Brightening my imagination,
Who hopes to possess you?
Not me.
You are like the moon in the distant sky,
Pleasant, cool, soothing,
But not for me,
A faint hope lingers,
Life is magic,
Life is miracle, you never know!
Then the universe will be mine.

□□□□

Are You Listening?

Just a call my heart gives you,
Though I have tried to curb it,
I have myself refused to listen,
My lips I have sealed tightly,
Imprisoned in an ivory tower,
Secluded, distanced from the world,
Outside is a facade of happiness,
A semblance of exuberance,
Still it is in the air,
    That mystic call,
        From heart to heart,
            Are you listening?

□□□□

A
Q
F
K
h
n
S
R
LOVE

Lost Love

Your name written on a yellowing page,
Takes me straight to you,
With hands entwined,
A smile on the lips,
Humming a tune,
Near a mountain ravine,
Watching the last sunset together,
We had promised to meet again,
Sometimes,
Fragrant breeze reminds me,
Of the promises you made
Though far away you went
I dream you still are mine,
Wistful smile erases,
The years in between
That without you I spent,
With just hope
And a few useless tears,
I wonder where does the love go,
That promises to stay for many births,
What remains is a blasted heart,
And a few pages,
With your name, written all over,
Unable to love again.

□□□□

Mother You Are Still With Me

I talk to you in inaudible whispers,
Weighed with stress and pain of life,
Who else will listen or understand?
Who else will lend a helping hand?
Only a mother can feel the pinch,
Of a daughter's anguished heart,
Ages have gone by since we met last,
Even in sorrow my life moved so fast,
My youthful face getting lines of stress,
Eyes becoming moist when grief I suppress,
When summoned from above you quickly went,
Living amongst angels where you were meant,
Now you are the moon that brightens my sky,
Amidst tumultuous storms my soul can spy.
Your love glows to guide my treacherous way,
A pillar of strength when the mind did sway
Each dawn brings warmth to wrap my weary soul,
Illuminating darkest night, warming frozen day,
When you are no more in this fickle world,
Your songs from around can still be heard,
I listen to birds when they come to wake me,
With mellifluous melodies just as yours,
Still listening to tales of my joys and woes.

□□□□

Language of Music: An Ode

An echo from the mountains,
A mellifluous strain,
Wafted in the air
A voice so magical that she stood in tracks,
Someone singing of Ranjha, the eternal lover,
Pining for Heer, his beloved,
Each strain captured the longing,
As if he himself was Ranjha,
Drenched in love's insatiable thirst,
Imploring God for final tryst with her,
Before he could die peacefully,
And stay forever with her.

Ranjha, whose call to cattle appeared like a peacock's call,
While in a graceful rhythm trying to please his beloved,
Playing upon his Vanjhali, he mesmerised the world,
She waited at the bend, sitting on a huge stone,
For the ravishing runes wouldn't let her move,
Enchanted by the mesmerising music,
Forgot where she was,
On the side of treacherous track,
All alone as she lagged behind,
While the entire group had moved on

Then the singing stopped, he appeared,

The whole world stood still,
Only their hearts sang,
Unstoppable,
Mellifluous, sonorous music,
Bewildered she tried to hush,
The rocks listened, pines moved, flowers smiled,
Now she knew, she herself was … Heer.

□□□□

Eventide

The exhausted sun watches the vale.
With closing eyes over the dale,
Has spilt his platter
All colours scatter
Apes chatter
Mystic tale
Silhouettes slowly merge with night,
Moon now shows her countenance bright,
White jasmines bloom
Sweet heady perfume
Expunges gloom
Perfect sight
Time to say farewell to sweet day
Leaving behind mellifluous lay
Flies in meadows green
Near hilly ravine now unseen,
Calm eventide of human life
Serene sober forgetting strife,
Wrinkles on the face,
Yet with divine grace,
Slowing pace virtues rife

□□□□

Where Has The Love Gone?

Nights move slowly without any sound,
With stark loneliness swathed around,
But from whence comes all this noise,
Of broken pieces of hope and disquiet,
I lie awake at nights thinking of you,
Wondering why your memories won't go,
Kept like ornaments in the cotton wool,
Tantalising dreams of love so cool!
Ages have gone by since met we last,
Faint fragrance still lingers in my heart,
Love in your eyes was just a beguile,
Was it just a fake, your alluring smile?
I didn't bother about the people around,
Sharp stares I ignored for love profound,
Your receding figure I still can spy,
Hoping you to turn and see me cry,
Your ego refused to share my woes,
Since then, silence has entered my life,
Quietly I watch my days go by.
Wavering amongst hope and strife.

□□□□

Farewell

I knew you were sick but that much!
Eyes gave recognising flicks,
A bubbly girl lying helpless as such,
Body bearing a dozen pricks,
White as lily was your delicate hand,
Almost drained of life,
My mind our entire lifetime spanned,
Once with joy that was rife
Tears trickled unabated as I did stand,
Prayers unanswered remained
For you were heading to Elysian land,
Where only bliss reigned,
Holding your hand I stood helpless and pained,
Contemplating each moment your memory contained.

□□□□

Vignettes of Life

Behold, a wallflower half hidden by stone,
But not without sharp prickly thorns
That sometimes make negligent passersby
Stop and look at what nature adorns,

Look! A twilight of blushing shades of red,
Awaiting dark night full of shining stars.
A nimble mountain river falling from the cliff,
Or an unhurried stream with a languid skiff,

Watch! A rebel trying hard to change,
A stubborn crowd, a surging mob,
A helpless coward watching with disdain,
Barbaric acts of violence causing bane,

Discern! An amalgam of emotions wild,
A drop of nectar with tears of pain,
Though hurt it is a thousand times,
Still loves with passion, a silly heart arcane.

View! A broken hut in desolate valley,
With flowery creepers overgrown, rife,
Having the best and the worst imaginable,
Playing with jest the game called life.

□□□□

Women and War

Monstrous wars perpetrate unending sufferings,
Wiping humans and humanity from the earth's surface,
Hark! Female voices praying for peace,
Their sighs and sobs pierce the streets,
They cry for dear ones wasted in the wars,
Listen to the helpless groans and shrieks,
For mutilated bodies and souls with scars,
Peaceful homes get drenched with gore.
Narcissistic ego, hunger for power comes to fore,
A Florence Nightingale then works tirelessly,
When war razed devastated land cries desperately.
Guileless people are thrown in the furnace of war.
They maintain those peaceful places of love, faith,
Abodes that take years to become homes,
Lie as heaps of ashes, unwept tombs,
Mothers waiting with vacant eyes at the thresholds,
Pay for narcissistic leaders' honour and ego untold,
Capable of bearing untold miseries,
These tender souls carve for peace,
Where is their voice in decision making?
Neglected half of humanity bears the brunt,
Of follies and foibles of those in front.

□□□□

Strange Passions

Dumbfounded I remain,
At the surge of love,
As a bellow strong,
Sweeps the shore,
Like a musk deer.
Searching from within,
Unable to gauge,
Passions unknown,
It has left me,
Mesmerised and dumb,
As if under a magic spell,
If I loved you less,
I would talk about it more,
Just peep into my eyes,
To get a glimpse,
Of love in my soul.

□□□□

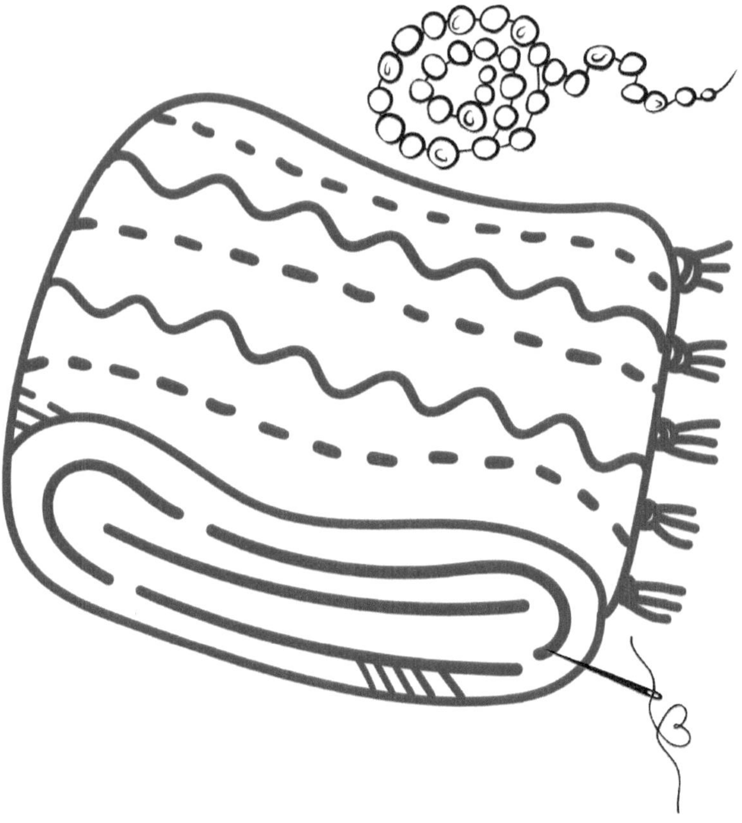

Moments

Every moment counts,
When knit together,
They form life,
Just as each drop of water combines,
To form ocean with waves high,
Moments are pearls joined together,
Some are beautiful, some maybe crooked,
Some are of cheers and some of tears,
Yet, significant in their own way,
Some ordinary looking, routine, boring,
Others threatening or life changing,
Moments spent in gruelling labour,
Moments wasted in useless clamour,
All form memories cherished later.
Each moment precious, don't let it go,
We never know when away it will flow.

□□□□

Horizon

Running through the *sarson* field,
We, the children could clearly see a space,
Where cerulean sky touched yellow flowers,
And there was a race to touch the place,
How innocent is the childhood never knowing,
That horizon will move farther and farther,
Like our impossible dreams and unfulfilled desires,
Yet every morning we climb the rock to watch,
Changing colours of the horizon from the top,
Ultimately the brilliant red sun will show,
Slowly changing hues from orange to yellow,
While mountains or trees stand silhouetted,
Or the outlines of flying birds are spotted.

□□□□

Sarson: Mustard

Eloquent Eyes

I know your secret.
You can hide from the world,

But your eloquent eyes speak,
Not a single secret, they can keep,
They sparkle with life as he arrives,
Brimming with cheer,

They don't need words,
To expose your heart's latent desire,

You hardly speak about it,
Yet love's fragrance can't hide.

□□□□

Vagrant Mind

My mind wanders
From place to place,
Along with the caravan of thoughts,
Like a gypsy woman
Tending her sheep,
Climbing the mountains,
Cooking food in earthenware,
Building a fire out of twigs
Singing a wild song of longing
Or of romance
It stays not at one place
Restless, agitated moves on,
Sometimes seen splashing water,
In a shallow river where silver fish jump
And plop back,
Or watching twinkling stars flowing
Down the stream
Laughing with the zephyrs
With thunder it screams
Gets lost in layers of time
Humming a forgotten rhyme
Of years bygone!

□□□□

Oh, My Desires!

On a lazy Sunday morning,
Unable to decide,
Whether I should sleep a bit more,
To let the nightly dream finish,
Or let it remain so that I can,
Imagine finishing it the way I like,
Or get out and watch,
New hibiscus flowers bloom,
Have a stroll in the cool October breeze,
Or click a few pictures of the sleepy larva,
Ready to pupate, before
It emerges as a shining butterfly,
Or hear the new song,
Bulbul has created for relaxed morning,
Or meditate to calm down agitating nerves,
Oh, the temptations!
Endless and unique!
But your thought hovers,
More mesmerising than the world around,
So I shall sleep for a few moments again,
To fulfil my desire.
Of meeting you, love,
At least in the dream!

□□□□

Oxymoron

Pretty they would call me sarcastically,
But that I was pretty ugly,
In super haste shaped by God,
And thrown down in a hurry,
Grew up lonely in the crowd,
Little knowledge did I gain,
With weird wisdom and clumsy clarity,
An educated fool I remain,
Heard Nature's silence with soundless moan,
With negligent care slowly I had grown,
With mirthless smiles and hateful love,
Amongst barren woods and waterless spring
Dark days of sadistic joy lifeless existence bring.

□□□□

Lessons of War

Vast demolished land of Kalinga,
With bodies strewn in the battlefield,
A beautiful land razed to ground,
By 'The Brave' King Ashoka, the great.
But he felt the pain and detested himself,
For all the destruction his ego caused.
Brave he was who left the war,
To spread a message of peace around
Brave is the tiny voice against injustice,
Standing with the oppressed during thick and thin,
Courage to stand against the bully,
A fight to ensure rights of the weak.

□□□□

The Unsung Songs

With parched throat and cracking voice,
I tried to sing the song of life,
Where love abounds and happiness reigns,
But no words came out of my mouth,
Those whom I loved deserted me,
Turned the life into a fearful farce,
Snatched my happiness with their lies,
Just to keep up an honest face,
My rhythm broke, the music faded,
Into the darkest recesses of soul,
Frozen along with grief of betrayal,
Shattering my belief in humanity all,
Song of peace remained unsung,
Tear choked throat lost its voice,
Deep wounds inflicted on my mind,
Took away melodies of every kind.

□□□□

The Melody of Heart

Adulation or abomination, intense pain or joy,
Turn sensitive heart palpable, creating verses,
A slight touch at the heart strings can create,
Mellifluous lays that spread like fragrant waves,
Tiny ripples of feelings can stir the entire ocean,
Sound wafts to the heaven bringing divine blessings,
A thought, a feeling, a word, a sound slowly moulds itself,
Drop by drop flows from the mind, on to the blank page,
Soon starts flowing as the melodious stream of poesy,
Floating in the air gracefully like colourful birds out of cage

□□□□

Red

I am the fierce red,
Colour of blood, colour of fire,
A volcano spewing endless anger,
Over injustices, crimes,
Perpetrated on the helpless,
Colour of roses gifted to lovers,
That seep their fragrance,
Into the crumbling pages,
Of old notebooks,
I am the rising sun,
Ushering another beautiful day,
I am the setting sun
Exhausting my last drop of brilliance,
Before going to sleep,
I am vermilion,
Embellishing her forehead,
I am the last drop of blood,
Used to revive a dying patient,
I am the blush on the face,
When lovesick ardent eyes steal a look.

□□□□

Advent of Spring

Spring slowly woke up in the white expanse,
Taking cold winter in the loving embrace,
"*Dearest here I am to realise your dreams,*"
Fulfil all promises you preserved so far,
Under the pristine cover of downy snow,
I will unveil the loveliest flowers,
Bring out fragrance and music of the nature,
That hibernated and rested because of winter,
To rejuvenate to its full glory and hope.

As you view the glorious sun,
Hearken to the sounds and songs without words,
The warmth and love have the hearts melted,
Just like snow as the golden orb appears,
Waking up bears and foxes from long siesta,
Watch sparrows return to their usual spirits,
Each verdure branch sprouting new life,
Flower buds have painted the valley flamboyant,
Odoriferous breeze has divulged loud and clear,
Goodbye winter, spring is here!

About the Poet - In Her Own Words

Perhaps the poet in me was always there — scribbling on the last pages of my notebook, trying to write what I felt at a particular moment or about a person around me. A joy I felt, a tear I controlled. Then there came diary writing — a mundane, day-to-day description of events, hiding my intimate feelings for the fear someone would read it. It wasn't about language or style; it was about my feelings.

I was too scared to show them. I don't remember how many words expressed me — in the form of stories, quotes, or just comments — were written and erased. I don't remember how many diaries I destroyed for fear that someone would read them. Then came social media, where I felt I could be invisible. My friends and family wouldn't know what I was writing, and they actually didn't know for years.

I remember my first temptation to add a couplet to the ghazal of a famous poetess, who appreciated it and sent a friend request — and I was too afraid to accept it. It was with disbelief that people accepted me as a writer and poet. Not that I am good at it, but now I have a voice. And here I am, with my first book of poetry — made possible by my new friends.

My poems are my smiles or tears in written form.

www.ingramcontent.com/pod-product-compliance
Lightning Source LLC
Chambersburg PA
CBHW022158160726
48282CB00024B/242
* 9 7 8 8 1 9 8 4 3 1 2 7 1 *